G000118042

US Air Power in colour 1

Robbie Shaw

Copyright © Jane's Publishing Company Limited 1987

First published in the United Kingdom in 1987 by
Jane's Publishing Company Limited
238 City Road, London EC1V 2PU

ISBN 0 7106 0431 9

All rights reserved. No part of this publication may be
reproduced, stored in a retrieval system, transmitted in any
form by any means electrical, mechanical or photocopied,
recorded or otherwise without prior permission of the
publisher.

Printed in the United Kingdom
by Netherwood Dalton & Co Ltd, Huddersfield

JANE'S TRANSPORT PRESS

Right: An F-15C of the 44th TFS, 18th TFW, holding for a "last
chance" check by groundcrew before lining up for take-off from its
base at Kadena. The 18th TFW has three F-15 squadrons — the
12th, 44th and 67th — and maintains a permanent detachment at
Osan in South Korea, where the Eagles augment the permanently
based F-4 Phantoms in the air defence role.

Cover illustrations

Front: Phantom! To some it's ugly, to others it's a work of art. But
everyone agrees that the big McDonnell Douglas type is a
magnificent fighting machine. The sheer power of the F-4 is
evident in this shot, taken during a flyby in afterburner at the
Imperial War Museum's Duxford airfield. This aircraft, RF-4C
68-565/AR, is from the 1st TRS, 10th TRW, at nearby
Alconbury. Note the arrester hook in the down position.

Back: The far from photogenic European 1 "lizard" camouflage is
spreading like wildfire among the USAF's squadrons. Once
resplendent in a gloss-white finish, the C-141B Starlifter fleet is
now wearing this toned-down scheme. Photographed at Kadena,
Okinawa, is aircraft 70009 from the 63rd MAW at Norton AFB,
California.

Introduction

Like many British aviation enthusiasts, I have grown up with a keen interest in the United States Air Force, the largest and most powerful air arm in the West, if not the world. As a schoolboy I saved my pocket money for a monthly visit to Prestwick, which in those days was home to a squadron of C-54 Skymasters. There I used to spend hours watching the transiting C-97 Stratocruisers, C-124 Globemasters and many others: if only I had had a camera then!

Now an air traffic controller in the Royal Air Force, I have often found myself working alongside USAF personnel. This in turn has meant that I have been perhaps better placed than civilian photographers to cover USAF aircraft, for which I am grateful.

In this book I have tried to cover most of the aircraft in the current USAF inventory, omitting only a few miscellaneous second-line types. I would like to thank the many base public affairs officers and staff members who have been of great assistance to me, in particular the PAO staff at HQ PACAF, 5th AF, 7th AF, Hickam AFB and Kadena AB. I also thank Gp Capt Milligan, Commander, Royal Air Force Hong Kong, for his support for this project, and Brendan Gallagher at Jane's for his faith in me.

The photographs in this book were taken with a pair of Pentax ME-Super bodies, Pentax 40.80mm zoom, 135mm and 200mm lenses, a Hoya 400mm lens, and Kodachrome 64 film.

ROBBIE SHAW
June 1987

The Rockwell B-1B supersonic swing-wing bomber is now in operational service with Strategic Air Command's 337th BS, 96th BW, at Dyess AFB, Texas. Illustrated here is B-1B 84-0050, belonging to the 6512th Test Squadron at Edwards AFB, California. A few B-1Bs remain assigned to Edwards for continuing trials of the aircraft and its systems. Note the large bomb-bay doors and the size of the flaps.

Abbreviations

AAS	Aeromedical Airlift Squadron
AAW	Aeromedical Airlift Wing
AB	Air Base
ABW	Air Base Wing
ACCS	Airborne Command and Control Squadron
AFB	Air Force Base
AFCC	Air Force Communications Command
AFFTC	Air Force Flight Test Centre
AFRES	Air Force Reserve
AFSC	Air Force Systems Command
ALCM	Air Launched Cruise Missile
ANG	Air National Guard
ARG	Air Refuelling Group
ARRS	Aerospace Rescue and Recovery Squadron
ARRW	Aerospace Rescue and Recovery Wing
ARS	Air Refuelling Squadron
ARW	Air Refuelling Wing
AS	Aggressor Squadron
ASD	Aerospace Systems Division
ATC	Air Training Command
AWCS	Airborne Warning and Control Squadron
AWCW	Airborne Warning and Control Wing
BS	Bombardment Squadron
BW	Bombardment Wing
CG	Composite Group
COIN	counter-insurgency
DACT	dissimilar air combat training
ECM	electronic countermeasures
ECS	Electronic Countermeasures Squadron
ECW	Electronic Countermeasures Wing
ELINT	electronic intelligence
FAC	forward air controller
FCS	Facility Checking Squadron
FIG	Fighter Interceptor Group
FIS	Fighter Interceptor Squadron
FITS	Fighter Interceptor Training Squadron
FLIR	forward-looking infra-red
FTS	Flying Training Squadron
FTW	Flying Training Wing
FWW	Fighter Weapons Wing
LORAN	Long Range Air Navigation (navigation system)
MAC	Military Airlift Command
MAS	Military Airlift Squadron
MAW	Military Airlift Wing
NAS	Naval Air Station
NASA	National Aeronautics and Space Administration
PACAF	Pacific Air Forces
RS	Reconnaissance Squadron
RW	Reconnaissance Wing
SAC	Strategic Air Command
SAM	surface-to-air missile
SOG	Special Operations Group
SOS	Special Operations Squadron
SOW	Special Operations Wing
SRS	Strategic Reconnaissance Squadron
SRW	Strategic Reconnaissance Wing
SW	Strategic Wing
TAC	Tactical Air Command
TACG	Tactical Air Control Group
TACW	Tactical Air Control Wing
TASS	Tactical Air Support Squadron
TAW	Tactical Airlift Wing
TFG	Tactical Fighter Group
TFS	Tactical Fighter Squadron
TFTS	Tactical Fighter Training Squadron
TFW	Tactical Fighter Wing
TG	Test Group
TRG	Tactical Reconnaissance Group
TRS	Tactical Reconnaissance Squadron
TRW	Tactical Reconnaissance Wing
TS	Test Squadron
TTW	Tactical Training Wing
USAF	United States Air Force
USAFE	United States Air Forces Europe
USMC	United States Marine Corps
USN	United States Navy
WRG	Weather Reconnaissance Group
WRS	Weather Reconnaissance Squadron

A-7D 72-0231 of the 120th TFS, 140th TFW, Colorado ANG, peels away after a mid-Atlantic refuelling from a KC-135A en route to its home base, Buckley AFB, after a European deployment. A-7 units regularly make use of tanker support to take part in exercises in Europe, where they would operate in large numbers in the event of war.

The Vought A-7 Corsair II, affectionately known as the SLUF ("Short Little Ugly Fella"), is derived from the larger F-8 Crusader. Designed initially as a carrierborne attack aircraft for the USN, the Corsair II entered Air Force service as the A-7D and saw action with TAC in Vietnam. Although subsonic, this robust little aircraft can deliver a weapon load very accurately: most A-7Ds have been fitted with the Pave Penny laser target-designation pod, and some aircraft also have forward-looking infra-red. A more recent addition to the inventory is the two-seat A-7K combat-capable trainer. Initially all A-7Ks were delivered to the 152nd TFTS of the Arizona ANG, the training unit for the type; subsequently each squadron has received a single A-7K. Aircraft from three squadrons deployed to RAF Waddington in 1985: 71-0295/IA of the 124th TFS, 132nd TFW, Iowa ANG, rotates **below** while A-7K 80-0292/SD of 175th TFS, 114th TFG, South Dakota ANG, flares before landing **right**.

Almost the whole of the Corsair fleet is assigned to the Air National Guard, equipping 12 ANG squadrons. One TAC unit, the 4450th TG at Nellis AFB, Nevada, uses the type for weapons trials, while the 6512th TS at Edwards AFB operates a number of A-7Ds, including some pre-production aircraft. These examples are painted white overall with dayglo orange fin and outer wings, as seen here on 68-8222/ED.

Winner in a flyoff against the Northrop A-9, the Fairchild A-10A Thunderbolt II was procured to replace the A-7 in the close support role with TAC. Regarded by some as one of the ugliest aircraft ever built, and nicknamed "Warthog" or just "Hawg", the A-10 is a potent tank-killer. Its GAU-8 30mm seven-barrelled cannon fires a phenomenal 4,200 rounds a minute, and 11 pylons can carry a variety of stores, including cluster bombs, Maverick missiles, fuel tanks and ECM pods. Illustrated here, devoid of external stores, is A-10A 81-0960/WR of the 81st TFW.

The A-10 is operated worldwide by the USAF. The largest wing is the 81st TFW, with six squadrons based at RAF Bentwaters and RAF Woodbridge. Within TAC it equips the 23rd and 354th TFWs, the 355th TTW and the 57th FWW. In addition, the 18th TFS at Eielson AFB, Alaska, and the 25th TFS at Suwon, South Korea, operate the type. All USAF A-10s are painted in the extremely effective European 1 "lizard" camouflage. **Left** TAC A-10A 78-0675/MB of the 356th TFS, 354th TFW, stands on the flight line at its base, Myrtle Beach, South Carolina. **Above** The tail code "SU" identifies A-10 80-0242 as belonging to the 25th TFS, 51st TFW, based at Suwon AB in South Korea.

The A-10 was the first front-line combat aircraft to be delivered directly from the factory to ANG and AFRES units. These aircraft, like the USAF's A-7s, regularly deploy to Europe, though their low speed makes them unpopular with tanker crews on such long journeys. AFRES A-10A 77-0267/NO, belonging to the 706th TFS, 926th TFG, at New Orleans NAS, Louisiana, is seen here with a Maverick missile under the port wing.

Strategic Air Command's newest asset, the Rockwell B-1B supersonic bomber, is now in service with the 96th BW at Dyess AFB, Texas, and the 28th BW at Ellsworth AFB, South Dakota. A total of 100 aircraft are currently on order for SAC, though Rockwell is trying hard to convince the USAF to buy more to replace the B-52s still in service. This is however unlikely to happen as the Advanced Technology Bomber (ATB) employing Stealth technology is due to enter service in the 1990s to replace the B-52 and complement the B-1B, which is still having teething problems, including fuel leaks. Photographed at Edwards AFB in fully swept configuration is B-1B 84-0050 of the 6512th TS.

Although the B-1B is smaller than its B-52 predecessor, it can carry a heavier weapon load and a wider variety of stores in its three bomb bays. The new bomber's airframe shaping, non-reflective paint scheme and other technological advances give it a radar signature only a fraction of that of the B-52. Combined with its offensive avionics and ECM equipment, this high degree of stealth greatly improves the B-1B's chances of survival as it penetrates heavily defended airspace, terrain-following at supersonic speeds. The crew of two pilots and two systems operators are accommodated in individual ejection seats, fitted in preference to the escape capsule which malfunctioned in the fatal crash of one of the prototypes. Illustrated is B-1B 84-0057 of the 6512th TS at Edwards AFB.

The heavyweight of manned bombers, the Boeing B-52 Stratofortress was conceived as long ago as 1946 and is still in the SAC inventory in large numbers. Equipping no fewer than 13 wings within SAC, this eight-engined leviathan will eventually be replaced by a combined force of B-1Bs and ATBs, the latter probably designated B-2. The B-52 fleet is currently receiving a new low-visibility paint scheme similar to that of the B-1B, which will help reduce the big bomber's radar signature. Illustrated in the new scheme is B-52G 80255 of the 60th BS, 43rd SW, the only B-52 unit based outside the continental US, at Anderson AFB, Guam.

Two variants of the BUFF ("Big Ugly Fat Fella"), the B-52G and B-52H, remain in service. A total of 90 of the former have been converted to carry ALCMs, and when B-1B deliveries are complete some B-52Hs will also be converted to this role. The first unit to be so equipped was the 668th BS, 416th BW, at Griffiss AFB, New York. B-52G 92601 from that squadron is illustrated **left**. B-52Gs not configured as ALCM-carriers have been equipped for the anti-shipping role with mines and Harpoon missiles; these aircraft equip the 42nd BW and 43rd SW. With the aid of in-flight refuelling the B-52 can deploy to any corner of the globe, as demonstrated by this shot **right** of a B-52G of the 69th BS, 42nd BW, refuelling from a KC-135 tanker over the UK, a long way from its home, Loring AFB, Maine.

15

The McDonnell Douglas F-4 Phantom II multi-role fighter joined the USAF in 1972 in the form of 30 US Navy aircraft on loan until the F-4C could be delivered in quantity. The Phantom served with distinction in South-east Asia, where it was operated in large numbers. The type continues to equip many units in TAC, USAFE, PACAF, ANG and AFRES, and is likely to remain in service into the next century, particularly in its F-4E form. This aircraft, F-4E 74-1633/SP of the 23rd TFS, 52nd TFW, is seen on take-off in strong crosswinds at RAF Sculthorpe.

The F-4D was the second Phantom variant to enter USAF service. It introduced major systems changes, including new weapon-ranging and release computers to increase accuracy in both the air-to-air and the air-to-ground roles. The F-4D bore the brunt of air combat in Vietnam, and a number of examples — distinguished by aerials on the fuselage spine — were equipped with LORAN for improved navigation in the region. The F-4D is now operated only by the AFRES and ANG. F-4D 40970 of the 178th FIS, 119th FIG, North Dakota ANG, seen here at Tyndall AFB, Florida, is used as an interceptor.

At one time the F-4C equipped no fewer than 16 of TAC's 23 wings. During the late 1960s a small number of F-4Cs were converted to Wild Weasel configuration for SAM-suppression duties, and some equipped the 81st TFS, 52nd TFW, at Spangdahlem until the arrival of the F-4G. But now only the ANG operates this variant, which is being progressively withdrawn from service. Many redundant F-4Cs are finding their way to USAF units worldwide for use as battle-damage repair airframes. Some ANG units are re-equipping with the F-4D and E, while others are upgrading even further, to the F-15 and F-16. One unit now in the process of receiving the Eagle is the 199th FIS, Hawaii ANG, based at Hickam AFB. Seen taxiing out **left** at that base is F-4C 63-7585, carrying the European 1 colour scheme, while **above** aircraft 37578 sports the newer Egypt 1 finish, now favoured for air defence units.

Above The F-4E, built in greater numbers than any other Phantom variant, introduced many improvements, including updated avionics and slatted wings for better manoeuvrability. It also featured a nose-mounted Vulcan 20mm cannon, and many examples were retrofitted with TISEO (Target Identification System Electro-Optical), an aid to the visual identification of targets. The type is now in ANG service, and also equips the 3rd TFW in the Philippines, 51st TFW in Korea, and the 52nd TFW at Spangdahlem in Germany. 74-0633/SP, from the 52nd's 81st TFS, is seen here at RAF Alconbury.

Right From the same McDonnell Douglas stable as the Phantom came the F-15 Eagle, designed to replace the F-4 in the air-superiority role. With pulse-Doppler radar and a maximum speed in excess of Mach 2, the F-15 is probably the best fighter in the world. The Eagle first flew on July 27, 1972, and the 1st TFW at Langley, Virginia, was the first operational unit to receive the type. Subsequent deliveries went to European-based units, the 36th TFW at Bitburg in Germany and the 32nd TFS at Soesterberg in Holland, both of which converted from Phantoms. F-15C 79-0023/CR of the 32nd TFS was photographed at RAF Alconbury.

The newer F-15 variants equip units in TAC, USAFE and PACAF, while the original F-15A is being introduced into the ANG as a replacement for F-4 Phantoms and F-106 Delta Darts. F-15s built from Fiscal Year 1978 onwards can carry FAST (Fuel and Sensor Tactical) Packs, mounted conformally next to the engine intakes and capable of almost trebling the internal fuel load. Aircraft thus equipped are designated F-15C, with the two-seat trainer version known as the F-15D. The Eagle normally carries a 600gal fuel tank on the centreline pylon, while armament includes a single M-61 20mm multi-barrel cannon mounted in the starboard wing root, four AIM-7 Sparrow medium-range air-to-air missiles and four short-range AIM-9 Sidewinders. The underwing pylons can also carry drop tanks, ECM pods or other ordnance. The F-15C equips the 1st and 33rd TFWs in TAC, 32nd TFS and 36th TFW in USAFE, the 57th FIS in Iceland, and the three squadrons of the 18th TFW at Kadena, Okinawa. The 18th's 44th TFS operates F-15D 78-0563/ZZ **left.** F-15C 78-505/ZZ of the 12th TFS **above** departs Kadena for a four-on-four engagement with Aggressor F-5s.

23

Although the F-15 has a respectable internal fuel load, like all USAF combat aircraft it is capable of being refuelled in flight by means of the receptacle in the port wing root. This capability is vital to the maintenance of effective combat air patrols. **Left** Contact! F-15C 78-0475/ ZZ of the 67th TFS, 18th TFW, receives the boom of a KC-135 tanker. **Right** Top-up complete, the Eagle "driver" slides away from the tanker to allow his wingman to take his place.

Left Despite the introduction of the F-15C, the F-15A still serves in large numbers with TAC units, including the 49th TFW, 325th TTW and 405th TTW, and the 5th FIS, 48th FIS and 318th FIS. Alaskan Air Command's 21st TFW also has one squadron. Photographed landing at RNAS Yeovilton is an F-15A of the Bitburg-based 36th TFW, which now flies the F-15C.

Below F-15s regularly participate in exercises throughout the USAF and NATO regions. One such is the twice-yearly Maple Flag, held at the Canadian Armed Forces base at Cold Lake, Alberta. Maple Flag is similar to the famous Red Flag exercises at Nellis AFB, which simulate operations against Warsaw Pact opposition. Exercise tasks for the Eagles include both the provision of top cover for attacking forces en route to the target, and combat air patrols to prevent attackers from reaching an objective. With its large airbrake extended, F-15C 82-0017/FF of the 27th TFS, 1st TFW, based at Langley AFB, Virginia, lands at Cold Lake.

F-15C 78-0514/ZZ of the 12th TFS, 67th TFW, leads as a pair of Eagles returns to base at Kadena, Okinawa. These aircraft had just spent 45 minutes engaged in intensive dissimilar air combat training with four F-5Es from the 26th Aggressor Squadron. The F-15's large canopy gives the pilot superb all-round vision in these encounters, which the USAF regards as essential to the training of effective fighter pilots.

The General Dynamics F-16 was born out of a USAF requirement for a new lightweight fighter. Two YF-16 prototypes were built to compete in a flyoff against the Northrop YF-17. After eleven months of intensive competition the F-16 was selected and named Fighting Falcon. As well as equipping many front-line squadrons, the F-16 also serves in both the ANG and AFRES, in many cases replacing the Phantom. It is armed with one fuselage-mounted M-61 cannon and can carry two wingtip-mounted missiles and seven stores pylons for ordnance, fuel and ECM pods. Powered by a single Pratt & Whitney afterburning turbofan producing 24,000lb of thrust, the F-16 is probably the most man-oeuvrable operational fighter in the world. In fact it can pull more g than a human pilot can tolerate, and it is believed that some F-16s have been lost because the pilot manoeuvred too violently and blacked out. F-16A 83-1114/MJ of the 13th TFS, 432nd TFW, is seen here landing at Misawa, Japan.

29

The first operational unit to receive the Fighting Falcon was the 388th TFW at Hill AFB, Utah. This wing comprises four squadrons, one of which was the initial training unit for the type. Next to equip was the 56th TFW at McDill AFB, Florida, which eventually took on the training role, using a number of F-16B two-seaters for this task. F-16Bs 78-0084 **above** and 78-0091/HL **right** of the 16th TFS, 388th TFW, were photographed at Hill AFB.

The F-16's outstanding manoeuvrability made it only a matter of time before the USAF's Air Demonstration Squadron, the Thunderbirds, converted to the Fighting Falcon. The red-white-and-blue aircraft of this unit are now regular performers at air shows around the USA, and they also toured Europe in 1984. A Far East tour, possibly including China, was on the cards for 1987. **Above** This Thunderbirds F-16A was seen at the Mildenhall Air Fete of 1984. **Right** Four of the team's six aircraft in tight formation over George AFB, California.

Developed from the F-102 Delta Dagger, the Convair F-106 Delta Dart entered USAF service in 1959 to provide air defence for the continental USA. Powered by a Pratt & Whitney J75 producing 24,500lb of thrust with afterburner, the Delta Dart has been regularly updated during its service life. Armament comprises a single M-61 cannon and four ageing AIM-4 Falcon missiles carried in an internal weapons bay. Compared with the F-15 and F-16, which are now replacing it, the F-106 appears dated, but its pleasing lines make it a favourite with aviation enthusiasts. Today only four units operate the Dart, three of them from the ANGs of Massachusetts, Montana and New Jersey. **Left** F-106A 72504, belonging to the 101st FIS Massachusetts ANG, was seen at Shearwater, Canada. **Above** The sole TAC operator is the 49th FIS, based at Griffiss AFB, New York, where 90074 was photographed.

The FB-111A is the medium-range strategic bomber version of General Dynamics' multi-role swing-wing aircraft. The type was procured for SAC as a replacement for the B-58 Hustler and early variants of the B-52. The FB-111A can carry four AGM-69 surface-to-air missiles on underwing pylons, with a further two in the bomb bay, or six nuclear weapons, or a mixture of nuclear and conventional ordnance up to 31,500lb. Two 500gal underwing drop tanks are normally carried. This type is operated by the 380th BW from Plattsburgh AFB, New York, and the 509th BW, based at Pease AFB, New Hampshire. Aircraft 80270 from the 380th BW was pictured at Shearwater, Canada.

Tactical Air Command uses two interdiction variants of the F-111. The F-111A equips the 366th TFW, based at Mountain Home AFB, Idaho, and the 27th TFW operates the F-111D from Cannon AFB, New Mexico. The F-111D has a European reinforcement role, and 68-0132/CC of the 522nd TFS, 27th TFW, was photographed during one such deployment. Note the empty bomb carrier under the port outboard pylon. Of the four underwing pylons, the two inner ones swivel as the wing sweeps, while the outboards are fixed and are loaded only when the mission permits the wing to be kept at an angle of 16°.

The F-111E and F forces are both based in Britain, the 20th TFW at RAF Upper Heyford and the 48th TFW at RAF Lakenheath. These aircraft are a vital asset to NATO in Europe, where they would be called on to carry out very difficult deep-penetration missions. Their ability to breach defences and find their targets was demonstrated during Operation El Dorado Canyon in 1986, when British-based F-111s reached Libyan targets undetected and bombed them with high accuracy. The F-111E's twin afterburning turbofans each produce 18,500lb of thrust, compared with the 25,100lb of the uprated engines fitted to the F-111F, which can also carry a Pave Tack laser target designator in its weapons bay. Both variants can carry two nuclear weapons internally and 25,000lb of various stores externally. An ECM pod is normally mounted underneath the rear fuselage, between the ventral fins. **Left** F-111E 68-0059/UH of the 77th TFS, 20th TFW, seen during a high-speed pass with wings swept fully back. **Right** On final approach to Alconbury is 70-2405/LN, an F-111F from the 494th TFS, 48th TFW.

The USAF's requirement for an airborne warning and control system (AWACS) led to development of the Boeing E-3 Sentry, essentially a Boeing 707 airframe with a Westinghouse look-down radar in a revolving radome mounted on the upper fuselage. This, along with an extensive suite of mission avionics, computers and data-processing equipment, provides TAC with a very effective mobile surveillance platform. A total of 34 aircraft have been built for the USAF's 552nd AWCW, based at Tinker AFB, Oklahoma.

The wing comprises six squadrons, two of which are based outside the US, one in Iceland and the other in Okinawa, Japan. Most of the aircraft delivered were E-3As, now being upgraded to E-3B standard, with improved avionics and better overwater radar performance. The later aircraft delivered were E-3Cs, with upgraded command and control facilities. **Left** E-3A 80576 of the 961st AWCS has just been pushed back into its Kadena revetment. **Above** E-3A 70355 of the 963rd AWCS lands at RAF Mildenhall.

41

Four Boeing 747 airframes were hardened against the electromagnetic effects of nuclear explosion and fitted with the most extensive communications equipment available to create the USAF's fleet of E-4B airborne command posts, one of which is earmarked as the National Emergency Airborne Command Post (NEACP). In time of tension the US President would make his decisions aboard an airborne E-4B orbiting in a remote area to avoid missile attack. All four aircraft are on the strength of the 1st ACCS at Offutt AFB, Nebraska, though one is always positioned at Andrews AFB, near Washington DC, ready for use by the President. The final E-4B built, 50125, is seen here at Fairford.

(Andy Thomson photograph)

One of the most easily identifiable of the many variants of the C-130 Hercules is the EC-130E Coronet Solo II electronic surveillance version, operated by the 193rd SOS, 193rd SOG, Pennsylvania ANG, based at Harrisburg Airport. This aircraft, serial number 39817, was seen arriving for the International Air Tattoo at Greenham Common. Note the large blade aerials on the wing undersurfaces and at the base of the fin.

The designation EF-111A Raven was applied to the 42 F-111As converted by Grumman for the defence-suppression role. EF-111A missions range from stand-off jamming to the escort of strike aircraft into the heart of enemy territory, jamming radar and radio communications to thwart the defences. Most of the aircraft's suppression systems, such as the ALQ-99 jammer, are carried internally. It is the ALQ-99 receivers that give the Raven its distinctive look, being mounted in a "football" at the top of the fin, as on Grumman's other electronic warfare type, the EA-6B Prowler. 67-0034/UH from the 42nd ECS, 66th ECW, based at RAF Upper Heyford, was photographed at RAF Fairford. The other EF-111A unit, the 390th ECS, is based at Mountain Home AFB, Idaho.

Although small numbers of F-4Cs were adapted for the Wild Weasel role, locating and destroying enemy radars, they were far from ideal for the task. As a result, 116 F-4Es were converted to F-4G Advanced Wild Weasel standard. Modifications included removal of the cannon and installation of AN/APR-38 electronics in its place, and the addition of a bullet fairing at the top of the fin. Once radar emissions have been detected, the F-4G can launch AGM-45 Shrike and AGM-88 HARM missiles which will home onto the source. F-4G 69-7212/SP from the 23rd TFS, 52nd TFW, was photographed at RAF Sculthorpe.

In USAFE all the Wild Weasels were initially concentrated in one squadron, the 81st TFS, 52TFW, based at Spangdahlem in Germany. They have since been distributed amongst all the squadrons in the wing, the others being the 23rd and 480th. The rest of the F-4G force is based at George AFB, California, home of the three squadrons — the 561st and 563rd TFS and 562nd TFTS — which make up the 37th TFW. The wing has been allocated the appropriate tail code "WW". **Below** F-4G 69-7561/WW, whose yellow fintip identifies it as belonging to the 561st TFS, was photographed at George AFB. The large missile on the inboard pylon is an AGM-45 Shrike. **Right** A close-up of the tail of 69-7288 from the 562nd TFTS shows the bullet fairing on the fin. Note also the Phantom "Spook" on the engine intake blanks.

The Boeing C-135 Stratotanker/Stratolifter has been developed into more variants than any other type in US service. Tasks include VIP transport, tanker, command post, ELINT, weather reconnaissance, and a wide variety of trials. The ELINT aircraft, designated RC-135U, V and W, are operated by the 55th SRW at Offutt AFB, Nebraska. Perman-ent detachments are maintained in Alaska, Greece, Japan and the UK, from which these electronic listening-posts operate to gather intelligence on Warsaw Pact communications and detection systems. **Above** On the approach to Mildenhall is RC-135V 39792. **Right** The many variants on the theme of the EC-135 airborne command post include the EC-135A, B, C, E, G, H, J, K, L, N, P, and Y! At least one of these aircraft is airborne at all times with a general and his battle staff on board. The only non-US-based EC-135 unit is the 10th ACCS, operating the EC-135H from RAF Mildenhall. One of this unit's aircraft, 10285, is seen here taxiing out for departure.

The versatile Phantom is also used by the USAF for all-weather photographic reconnaissance. Designated RF-4C, this unarmed version can go in fast and low, using its nose-mounted cameras to record the vital information required by battlefield commanders. Intelligence can also be returned near-instantaneously by means of data-link transmission. Some RF-4Cs are fitted with the Pave Tack infra-red pod, which allows targets to be located more readily, and the fleet is in the process of receiving smokeless engines, which will greatly increase their chances of survival against enemy air defences. Fourteen squadrons, including eight ANG units, are equipped with the RF-4C. **Left** Seen on the taxiway at its home base, Kadena, is 65-0940/ZZ of the 15th TRS, 18th TFW, the sole PACAF operator of the type. The unit has a permanent detachment at Osan AFB, South Korea. USAFE has two squadrons, at RAF Alconbury in Britain and Zweibrucken in Germany. The 1st TRS, 10th TRW, is based at Alconbury, where **below** 68-0561/AR was photographed taxiing clear of the runway with its brake 'chute streamed.

The Lockheed SR-71A Blackbird still makes enthusiasts stop and stare in awe. First flown in late 1964, the type is still cloaked in secrecy, and is the holder of many world records. Strategic reconnaissance is the mission of this phenomenal aircraft, which can fly at altitudes in excess of 80,000ft at Mach 3+, carrying a payload of highly sensitive sensors and cameras. The Blackbird is operated by the 1st SRS, 9th SRW, from Beale AFB, California. It is flown by a crew of two, comprising pilot and systems operator. Two variants are used for pilot training, the SR-71B and SR-71C, both of which have a raised rear cockpit to improve the instructor's view. The 9th SRW maintains two permanent detachments overseas, at Kadena AB, Okinawa, and RAF Mildenhall in the UK. **Below** The shockwaves from two engines generating 34,000lb of thrust each are evident in this shot of SR-71A 17979 departing RAF Fairford. **Right** This picture of 17976 landing at RAF Mildenhall ahead of an inbound storm is unusual in showing a full-colour 9th SRW badge on one fin.

Apart from the spectacular Blackbird, the 9th SRW at Beale AFB operates another high-flying, though much slower, reconnaissance aircraft, the Lockheed TR-1. Derived from the famous U-2, the type is currently in production for SAC, and 26 TR-1A single-seaters are believed to be on order. The majority are destined for Europe, tasked with all-weather battlefield surveillance using a comprehensive fit of electronic sensors, including side-looking airborne radar (SLAR). A number of TR-1s are due to be fitted with the Precision Location Strike System (PLSS), which would require three aircraft to work as a team to locate enemy emitters. Aircraft based in Europe are assigned to the 95th RS, 17th RW, at RAF Alconbury, where aircraft 01068 was photographed taxiing out **above** and on the approach **right**.

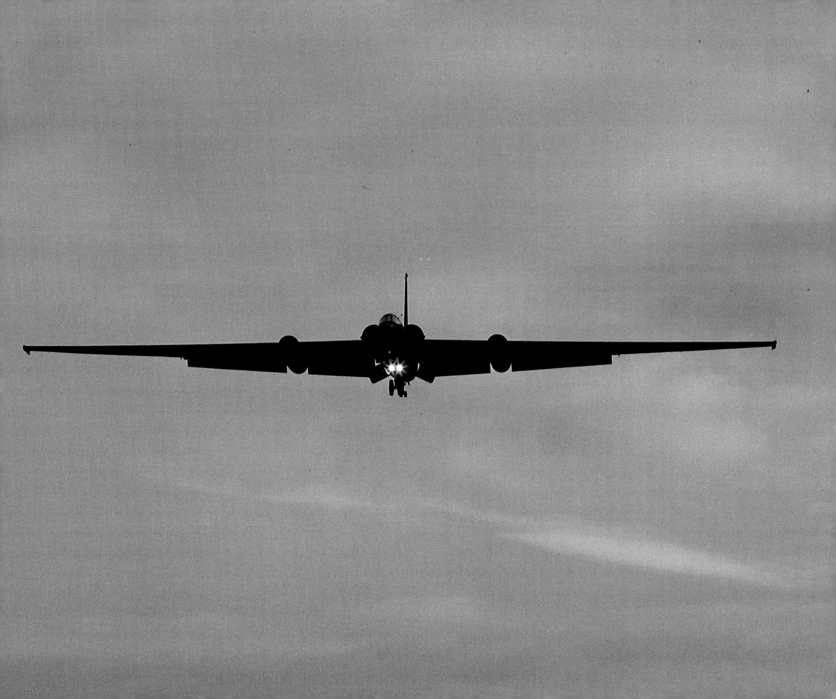

The TR-1 (pages 54 and 55) is an upgraded version of the U-2R, from which it is externally indistinguishable. The U-2R, built in the late 1960s, features a 25% increase in length and wing span compared with the earlier models of the U-2 family. It is believed that the initial U-2 variants have all been retired, leaving the U-2R and TR-1A to be operated by the 99th SRS from Beale AFB, California. **Left** TR-1A 01078 from the 95th RS, 17th RW, on final approach to RAF Alconbury. **Above** U-2R 10337 of the 99th SRS, 9th SRW, landing at RAF Mildenhall. Note the SLAR on the port wing pod.

The USAF takes weather reconnaissance very seriously, tasking no fewer than four squadrons with this duty. Often the most reliable way of forecasting the movement of severe weather fronts and tropical storms is to fly into them — not a job for the faint-hearted! It is standard practice for a weather reconnaissance aircraft to precede a fighter deployment by 24 hours, supplying information on which route plans can be based. For this task the MAC employs the WC-135Bs of the 55th WRS, based at McClellan AFB, California.

The other three weather recce units operate two Hercules variants, the WC-130E and WC-130H. The 53rd WRS, based at Keesler AFB, Mississippi, covers the Atlantic, while the 54th WRS at Andersen AFB, Guam, is responsible for the Pacific. Also located at Keesler is the 815th WRS, an AFRES squadron. One of the latter unit's aircraft, WC-130H 50967, is seen **left** at Keesler. **Above** WC-135B 12674 was photographed at RAF Alconbury. Note the scoop for collecting air samples on the side of the fuselage.

The largest aircraft in the USAF inventory, the Lockheed C-5 Galaxy long-range heavy transport was introduced into MAC service in December 1969. A total of 81 C-5As were eventually taken on charge. Some of these aircraft have since been handed on to the AFRES and ANG, equipping one unit each. Delivery of 50 C-5Bs is now under way. This variant is structurally identical to the C-5A, but features updated avionics and more powerful engines. The cavernous fuselage can accommodate two M-60 main battle tanks or three Chinook twin-rotor helicopters. Three MAC wings are equipped with the C-5, nicknamed "Fat Albert" by its crews. The 443rd MAW at Altus AFB, Oklahoma, is the training unit. Operational wings comprise the 60th MAW at Travis AFB, California, and the 436th MAW at Dover AFB, Delaware. **Left** C-5A 00463 of the 436th MAW climbs out of RAF Mildenhall. **Above** Brand-new C-5B 50002 from the 60th MAW approaches Hickam AFB, Hawaii.

61

The McDonnell Douglas DC-9 serves in the USAF, appropriately designated C-9. A total of 21 were taken on charge by MAC for aeromedical evacuation duties. These C-9A Nightingales are operated by the 375th AAW at Scott AFB, Illinois; 20th AAS at Clark AB in the Philippines; and 55th AAS at Rhein-Main, West Germany. Some aircraft from the latter unit have been converted into pure transports and are operated by the 7111th Operations Squadron. One of these, 10882, is seen here landing at RAF Mildenhall.

The Beech King Air 200 was initially purchased as an operational support and short-range transport, designated C-12A. In May 1984 MAC took delivery of a further 40 examples on a five-year lease with an option to buy that has since been exercised. Along with the C-21A these aircraft, designated C-12F, are due to replace the CT-39 Sabreliner. Further C-12Fs are to be acquired to replace the ANG C-131 fleet. Seen here is aircraft 40165, a C-12F of the Ramstein-based 58th MAS.

Left The Grumman Gulfstream 3, known as the C-20A in USAF service, was selected intially to supplement and eventually replace the C-140B JetStar in the VIP transport role. Three were bought for use by the 1st MAS, 89th MAW, at Andrews AFB, Maryland. The C-20's ability to fly non-stop across the Atlantic makes it particularly useful, and a further eight have been ordered, some of which will be assigned to the 58th MAS at Ramstein, Germany. C-20A 30502 is seen here sunning itself on the ramp at Hickam AFB, Hawaii.

Above Another recent business jet addition to the MAC fleet is the Gates C-21A Learjet high-speed communications aircraft. A total of 80 C-21s were leased for an initial five-year period, with an option to purchase which has since been taken up. Up to eight passengers can be carried by the C-21A, which has replaced the CT-39 Sabreliner in USAF service. In addition to US-based aircraft, two are located at Yokota, Japan, for use by PACAF, and a further six in Germany. 40081 of the Stuttgart-based 608th MAG was photographed at RAF Fairford.

Left The military derivative of the successful Shorts 330 feederliner is known as the Sherpa. A total of 18 C-23A Sherpas were acquired by the USAF to meet its European Distribution System Aircraft (EDSA) requirement. A further 48 examples remain under option. Assigned to the 10th MAS, 608th MAG, at Zweibrucken, West Germany, the C-23 is used on scheduled freight runs throughout the USAFE region, delivering spare parts to keep combat aircraft serviceability high. C-23A 40459 is seen on the approach to RAF Mildenhall.

Below The Lockheed C-130 Hercules has been the USAF's standard tactical transport since its introduction in 1956. Many variants of this workhorse are in current service, including gunship, ECM, rescue, special forces and weather reconnaissance versions. It is in use with MAC, TAC, AFRES and ANG. Indeed, new-build C-130Hs are still coming off the production line for AFRES and ANG. Some of the transport Hercules — like C-130E 21294 from the 314th TAW at Little Rock AFB, Arkansas, seen here landing at RAF Mildenhall — are painted in desert camouflage.

The Lockheed C-140A JetStar was introduced into USAF service in 1961, when five aircraft were purchased for the task of calibrating navigation and airfield approach aids. They were initially painted in a high-visibility colour scheme — needed for safety when operating in busy airspace — but for some reason now wear the much less suitable European 1 camouflage.

The four C-140As still in service are used for calibration checks at all military air bases in the USA, operating from Scott AFB, Illinois, with the 1866th FCS, AFCC. One of these aircraft, 95962, is illustrated **left**. A further eleven JetStars, designated C-140B, were procured as VIP transports and operated by the 89th MAW at Andrews AFB. Five of these aircraft

were later transferred to the 58th MAS at Ramstein, Germany. Both units still operate the JetStar, though in reduced numbers because some aircraft have been retired. The remainder will be replaced by the C-20A Gulfstream 3. **Above** C-140B 12491 of the 58th MAS was photographed at RAF Brawdy.

The Lockheed C-141A Starlifter was designed in the early 1960s to replace the USAF's fleet of piston-engined transports such as the C-118 and C-124. Four early examples are operated as NC-141As by AFSC at Wright Patterson AFB, Ohio, the remainder equipping six wings in MAC. The 443rd MAW at Altus AFB, Oklahoma, is the training unit for both the C-5 and C-141. On the west coast the 60th, 62nd and 63rd MAWs, based at Travis, McChord and Norton AFBs respectively, cover the Pacific area. The Atlantic and European theatres are the responsibility of the 437th and 438th MAWs at Charleston and McGuire AFBs respectively. In December 1979 the first of a stretched variant, the C-141B, entered service. The remainder of the fleet, with the exception of the AFSC aircraft, have since been converted to the standard. Two barrel sections were inserted into the fuselage, increasing its length by 23ft 4in, and a refuelling receptacle was installed above the cockpit. The C-141 is now entering service with the AFRES and ANG. C-141Bs 50239 of the 60th MAW **above** and 70009 of the 63rd MAW **right** were photographed at Kadena, Okinawa.

The McDonnell Douglas DC-10 was selected in preference to the Boeing 747 to meet a requirement for an Advanced Tanker/Cargo Aircraft (ATCA), intended primarily to supplement SAC's KC-135 force. Known as the KC-10A Extender, the aircraft has proved invaluable, combining the ability to refuel deploying fighter units while transporting their support equipment and ground crews at the same time. In addition to the standard USAF flying-boom refuelling system, the Extender also has a hose-and-drogue arrangement suitable for use with USN/USMC and NATO fighter aircraft fitted with probes. Well over half of the 60 aircraft on order have been delivered, equipping the 2nd BW at Barksdale AFB, Louisiana, 22nd ARW at March AFB, California, and the 68th ARG at Seymour Johnson AFB, North Carolina. Although these aircraft come under the operational control of SAC, they are often used purely in the passenger/freight role by MAC. When first delivered they sported gloss-white upper surfaces, blue cheatline and grey undersides, but more recent aircraft have a low-visibility finish of matt dark grey with light grey undersides. Two aircraft from the 32ARS, 2BW, are illustrated: aircraft 90434 **left** trails its hose and drogue, while 40192 **below** is in the low-visibility colour scheme.

A small number of C-135 Stratolifter VIP transports are in use with MAC and SAC. In addition, there are five similar aircraft, designated C-137, in service with the 89th MAW at Andrews AFB. These include "Air Force 1" and "Air Force 2" of the Presidential fleet. **Above** C-135C 12671 of Detachment 1 of the 89th MAW was photographed at Hickam AFB, Hawaii. Note the immaculate paint finish, the engine blanks with the inscription "Special Air Mission Hawaii", and the four stars. The most numerous C-135 variant is the KC-135 Stratotanker, of which over 700 were delivered to SAC in support of the manned bomber force and TAC fighter fleet. The KC-135A entered service in 1956, and now a programme of improvements looks likely to extend its life into the next century. AFRES and ANG aircraft are being re-engined with JT3D turbofans and redesignated KC-135E, while a further batch, to be redesignated KC-135R, are receiving the very fuel-efficient CFM56 powerplant.

Right KC-135E 71460 of the 117th ARS, 190th ARG, Kansas ANG, roars down the runway at RAF Scampton.

The task of the forward air controller (FAC) is dangerous but vital. His job is to find and identify a ground target, mark it with rockets, and then call in a strike force for the attack. He often comes under fire before the attack and when he goes back to assess the damage. For many years the mount of the USAF's FACs has been the Cessna O-2, a variant of the civil Cessna 337 Skymaster, which can carry rockets and a 7.62mm minigun. **Left** Seen at Davis-Monthan AFB, Arizona, is O-2A 10838 of the 23rd TAS, 602nd TACW. The O-2 is slowly being replaced by the OA-37B Dragonfly now that this type has been withdrawn from the ground attack role. The jet-powered Dragonfly is faster and more manoeuvrable than its predecessor, and has eight underwing pylons capable of carrying a variety of external stores. The 23rd TASS, based at Davis-Monthan AFB, has now relinquished its O-2s in favour of the OA-37B. One of the unit's new mounts, 31110/NF **below,** was photographed at George AFB, California.

The North American OV-10A Bronco is used for FAC and is also suitable for counter-insurgency, a role in which its four 7.62mm machine guns can be employed to good effect. Fuselage sponsons can carry up to 2,400lb of ordnance, including rockets and bombs, while a centre-line pylon normally accommodates an external fuel tank. US-based Bronco units comprise the 27th TASS at George AFB, California, the 22nd TASS at Wheeler AFB, Hawaii, and the 549th TASS at Patrick AFB, Florida, which also has O-2s. The sole non-US-based unit is the 19th TASS at Osan AB, South Korea. **Below** Seen here in "lizard" colours is OV-10A 83792 of the 19th TASS. **Right** In the more recent grey scheme is 03808/WH from the 22nd TASS.

Among the unsung heroes of the Vietnam War were the HH-3 helicopter crews who regularly flew deep into enemy territory to rescue downed aircrew. The HH-3 is a military version of the Sikorsky S-61, equipped with a nose-mounted retractable probe with which it can receive fuel from the HC-130 tanker. Nicknamed the "Jolly Green Giant", the type is still the mainstay of MAC's rescue squadrons. In addition, two units, including one from AFRES, fly the CH-3E for tactical support missions. Illustrated is HH-3E 14711 of Detachment 11, 38th ARRS, Myrtle Beach AFB, South Carolina.

Big brother of the HH-3, and derived from the Sikorsky S-65, is the H-53 "Super Jolly Green Giant" multi-role helicopter. USAF CH-53Cs based at Sembach in Germany are used in support of mobile tactical air control systems, while the much modified HH-53H is operated exclusively by the 20th SOS at Hurlburt Field, Florida, on Special Forces missions. The latter variant is equipped with forward-looking infra-red, permitting operations at night or in bad weather. The HH-53C is the standard rescue aircraft. Serving with the 67th ARRS at RAF Woodbridge, HH-53C 95784 is seen here on static display at RAF Greenham Common.

81

The famous Bell UH-1 Iroquois, better known as the "Huey," has been in USAF service for over 20 years. The twin-engined UH-1N is used primarily for rescue missions within easy reach of our bases, though some serve as VIP and general transports, and also operate with Special Forces. The single-engined HH-1H, the last Huey variant to be delivered, is used exclusively for base rescue. Earlier single-engined versions were the TH-1F, UH-1F and UH-1P. Small numbers of these aircraft are still on the active inventory, and are flown mainly in support of SAC's missile units, carrying personnel and cargo to remote sites.

Below UH-1N 96608, used by Detachment 2, 67th ARRS, at Ramstein, Germany, as a general and VIP transport. **Right** Showing no trace of its 20 years is an immaculate TH-1F, 61238 of the 35th TTW, pictured at its home base, George AFB, California.

The successor to the Northrop F-5A light export fighter is the F-5E Tiger II. A number of F-5Es and F-5F two-seat trainers are operated by the 425th TFTS, 405th TTW, at Williams AFB, Arizona, primarily for the training of overseas users of the F-5. At the time of the fall of South Vietnam, large numbers of F-5Es were on order for or awaiting delivery to the South Vietnamese Air Force. The USAF decided that these surplus aircraft, with their high manoeuvrability and MiG-like characteristics, would be ideal for dissimilar air combat training (DACT). It was found during the South-east Asian conflict that the majority of pilots shot down in combat suffered this fate early in their tour, usually within the first ten missions. DACT is intended to reduce that risk, familiarising pilots with the problems of combat by pitting them against US pilots flying the F-5 but using enemy tactics. The first unit to form in the DACT role was the 26th Aggressor Squadron (AS) at Clark AB in the Philippines. Seen here **above** and **right** is F-5E 01574 from that unit.

DACT F-5s are painted in a variety of colour schemes duplicating those of potential adversaries. The 26th AS provides DACT for PACAF-based units and is frequently "on the road," touring the various fighter bases to exercise with aircraft such as the F-4, F-15 and F-16. Today there are four Aggressor squadrons: the 26th; the 64th and 65th of the 57th FWW, based at Nellis AFB, Nevada, to work with US-located units; and USAFE's 527th AS. In addition to participation in Red Flag exercises at Nellis, the 64th and 65th visit US-based squadrons to preach the gospel of "check six". The 527th AS is based at RAF Alconbury and has a semi-permanent detachment at Decimomannu in Sicily, the NATO weapons range. Here they regularly pit their skills in the Air Combat Manoeuvring Instrumentation Range against pilots and aircraft from a variety of NATO units. It is expected that the F-5 will be replaced in a few years' time, probably by the F-16. **Below** F-5E 01568 of the 527th AS, seen at Alconbury. **Right** The 26th AS road show at rest during a visit to Kadena, Okinawa.

The USAF recently announced the imminent retirement of the Lockheed T-33A Shooting Star after nearly 40 years' service. Well over a hundred "T-Birds" are still in use, the majority with the 95th FITS, 325th FWW, at Tyndall AFB, Florida. Most US-based interceptor squadrons operate three or more of the type in a variety of roles, including target-towing, cruise missile simulation, and even air combat training. In the latter role the T-33 augments the F-5E with the 26th AS at Clark AFB in the Philippines. At Hickam AFB in Hawaii T-33s do the same job in support of the 199th FIS, as well as acting as training targets for air defence radar operators. The oldest T-Bird in USAF service, an NT-33A, is used as a trials aircraft by the AFFTC at Edwards AFB, California. **Above** T-33A 70686 of the 15th ABW was photographed at Hickam. Camouflaged T-33s are believed to be unique to this unit, which also has some aircraft in two-tone grey. **Right** 35900 is operated by the Tyndall-based 325th TTW.

Successor to the T-33 as Air Training Command's primary trainer was the Cessna T-37 "Tweety Bird". This side-by-side two-seat jet was introduced in 1956 as the T-37A and upgraded to T-37B standard from 1959. Over 600 T-37Bs equip eight training wings. A number of camouflaged examples have replaced the O-2 with the 21st TASS at Shaw AFB, South Carolina. At one time due for replacement by the subsequently cancelled Fairchild T-46A, the T-37 could now soldier on into the next century. Another possibility being urged by some members of Congress is a purchase of the British Aerospace Hawk, already selected by the USN. The first two T-46As underwent intensive flight trials at Edwards AFB before the programme was axed early in 1987. **Below** T-37B 81906 is operated by the 454th FTS, 323rd FTW, at Mather AFB, California, for navigator training. **Right** The second T-46A to be built, 84-493, is seen undergoing tests with the 6512th TS, AFFTC, at Edwards.

On completion of basic
flying training on the T-37,
USAF student pilots
switch to the Northrop
T-38A Talon for advanced
tuition. Almost identical to
the F-5B, the Talon equips
seven ATC wings and,
until replaced by the F-16,
was the mount of the
Thunderbirds aerobatic
team. Air Force Systems
Command trials units at
Eglin and Edwards AFBs,
and the civilian agency
NASA, use the type for
chaseplane duties, while
SAC's 9th SRW operates a
number for SR-71 pilot
proficiency flying. An
armed version with
gunsight and practice-
bomb dispensers, known as
the AT-38B, is flown by
the four squadrons of the
479th TTW from
Holloman AFB, New
Mexico. The wing's task is
to train pilots to use
aircraft as fighting
machines, teaching them
the rudiments of air
combat and air-to-ground
weaponry. **Left** Taxiing in
at Edwards is T-38A 10402
of the 6512th TS, AFFTC.
AT-38Bs of the 479th
TTW all wear a photo-
genic three-tone blue
camouflage scheme, as
modelled **right** by 13169/
HM, seen landing at NAS
Miramar, California. The
yellow band on the fin
identifies the aircraft as
belonging to the 463rd
TFTS.

Left Derived from the North American Sabreliner executive jet, the T-39 was bought by the USAF for pilot proficiency training, though its primary role soon became communications and VIP transportation. The type is now being phased out following the introduction of the C-12F and C-21A. Soon the only operational T-39s will be a handful at Wright-Patterson AFB, Ohio, with the Aerospace Systems Division of AFSC, and two calibration aircraft. The latter are operated by the 1867th FCS at Yokota, Japan, and 1868th FCS at Rhein-Main, Germany. Seen landing at RAF Mildenhall is 24453 from the 1868th FCS.

Above Navigator training is the responsibility of the 323rd FTW, flying T-37Bs and T-43As from Mather AFB, California. The latter type is a Boeing 737 airframe equipped with the avionics and navigation systems most commonly used by USAF aircraft. It is operated by the 455th FTS. Seen here is T-43A 11406 on the point of departing Edwards AFB as dusk approaches at the end of an air show.

In any air force the pilots and aircraft receive most of the acclaim. But it should not be forgotten that it takes many people on the ground to get an aircraft and crew into the air. The administrators sorting out pay and paperwork, the air traffic controllers in the tower, and the skilled technicians all have an important part to play in creating effective air power. Here, on the floodlit hardstanding of Yokota AB, Japan, C-130E Hercules of the 345th TAS, 316th TAG, are being readied for their next day's work.